On the Map

Mapmaking

Cynthia Kennedy Henzel

ABDO
Publishing Company

visit us at
www.abdopublishing.com

Published by ABDO Publishing Company, 8000 West 78th Street, Edina, Minnesota 55439.
Copyright © 2008 by Abdo Consulting Group, Inc. International copyrights reserved in all
countries. No part of this book may be reproduced in any form without written permission from the
publisher. The Checkerboard Library™ is a trademark and logo of ABDO Publishing Company.

Printed in the United States.

Cover Photo: iStockphoto
Interior Photos: Alamy p. 26; AP Images p. 16; Breton Littlehales/National Geographic Image
    Collection p. 19; Comstock pp. 25, 29; Corbis pp. 5, 8, 21, 27, 28; Getty Images pp. 10, 18;
    iStockphoto pp. 6, 11, 12, 13, 14; Library of Congress p. 9; U.S. Census Bureau p. 7;
    Visible Earth/NASA p. 15

Series Coordinator: BreAnn Rumsch
Editors: Megan M. Gunderson, BreAnn Rumsch
Art Direction & Cover Design: Neil Klinepier

Library of Congress Cataloging-in-Publication Data

Henzel, Cynthia Kennedy, 1954-
  Mapmaking / Cynthia Kennedy Henzel.
    p. cm. -- (On the map)
  Includes bibliographical references and index.
  ISBN 978-1-59928-950-2
  1. Cartography--Juvenile literature. I. Title.

  GA105.6.H47 2008
  526--dc22

               2007029203

Contents

Let's Make a Map

All kinds of people make maps! Explorers and adventurers map their discoveries. Pirates make treasure maps. Friends draw maps to give each other directions. And **cartographers** map everything from malls to the universe.

Maps are meant to communicate something about an area. So before beginning a map, a cartographer must first decide what information the map will communicate. The map's purpose will determine the area it covers.

One map's purpose may be to help students find a classroom. In this case, the cartographer must map the whole school. But perhaps the map just needs to show where a student sits. For this purpose, only one classroom needs to be mapped.

The purpose also determines what details a map shows. Maps are only representations of reality. So, a map does not show everything. A classroom map might show the desks, the sink, and the pencil sharpener. But, it probably will not show each pencil. Once you know the purpose of your map, you are ready to begin!

You can map anything around you, big or small. Will you map the whole world or just your neighborhood?

HUDSON
BAY

What Kind of Map?

Next, you will need to determine what kind of map you will make. Most maps fall into one of two categories. Your map will most likely be either a reference map or a thematic map.

A reference map gives a general idea of an area or helps people find their way around. You might draw a reference map of your neighborhood to show where your house is. Or, you might map your bedroom to show where your things belong.

A thematic map has a theme, or subject, as its main purpose. For example, a thematic map might show the number of classrooms with more boys than girls.

On a thematic map, groups of information called cohorts are assigned a color or a symbol. For example, the classrooms with more boys might be shaded blue. The classrooms with more girls

Maps can tell you about the people in your community.

might be shaded red. Those with an equal number of boys and girls might be shaded yellow.

After deciding whether your map will show a place or an idea, you will know what kind of information you need. Now it is time to gather the data!

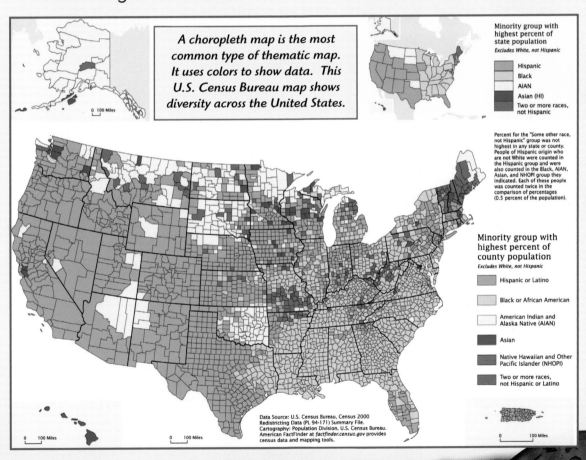

A choropleth map is the most common type of thematic map. It uses colors to show data. This U.S. Census Bureau map shows diversity across the United States.

Minority group with highest percent of state population
Excludes White, not Hispanic

- Hispanic
- Black
- AIAN
- Asian (HI)
- Two or more races, not Hispanic

Percent for the "Some other race, not Hispanic" group was not highest in any state or county. People of Hispanic origin who are not White were counted in the Hispanic group and were also counted in the Black, AIAN, Asian, and NHOPI group they indicated. Each of these people was counted twice in the comparison of percentages (0.5 percent of the population).

Minority group with highest percent of county population
Excludes White, not Hispanic

- Hispanic or Latino
- Black or African American
- American Indian and Alaska Native (AIAN)
- Asian
- Native Hawaiian and Other Pacific Islander (NHOPI)
- Two or more races, not Hispanic or Latino

Data Source: U.S. Census Bureau, Census 2000 Redistricting Data (PL 94-171) Summary File. Cartography: Population Division, U.S. Census Bureau. American FactFinder at *factfinder.census.gov* provides census data and mapping tools.

0 100 Miles

The Right Data

The next step in mapmaking is gathering information. When gathering information, **cartographers** use many sources. They take field measurements and gather **statistics**. Cartographers also use aerial photographs and **satellite** images.

Before a cartographer can create a reference map, a surveyor must measure the area to be mapped.

To gather information for a reference map, measurements must be taken. The cartographer needs to know the size of the area to be mapped. The size of the objects in the area and the distances between them also must be measured.

Your reference map can be either large **scale** or small scale. A large-scale map shows a small area in great detail. For example, a map of your classroom might be measured in feet or meters. A small-scale

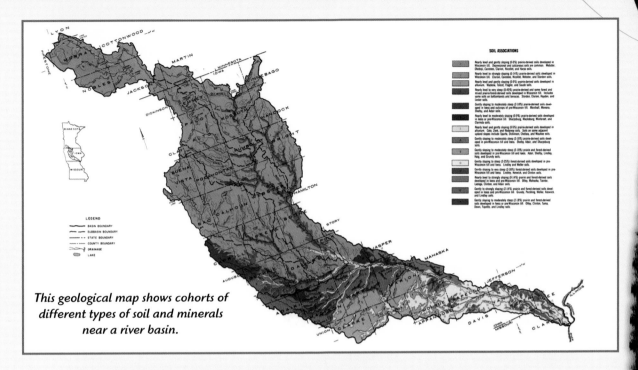

SOIL ASSOCIATIONS

This geological map shows cohorts of
different types of soil and minerals
near a river basin.

map shows greater areas in less detail. A world map is a
small-**scale** map. Distances on small-scale maps are often
measured in miles or kilometers.

For a thematic map, a **cartographer** needs to collect
information about the map's theme. Imagine you want to map
classes with a lot of school spirit. In this case, you might do a
survey. You could ask each student to rate their own school
spirit as Low, Medium, or High. Then, you could map these
cohorts using colors or symbols.

Mapmaking Tools

After collecting the information needed for your map, you must gather the tools to draw the map. First, choose what material the map will be drawn on. Heavy paper, cardboard, or plastic would be good choices for a wall map. Paper that is **durable**, yet easy to fold, would be the best choice for a road map.

The size and distance of things shown on a map should be **accurate**. To show these elements correctly, you will need tools for measuring. A ruler can measure distances on the map and draw straight lines. A calculator may help you determine the correct measurements.

The design of a map helps communicate information, too. You can use colored pencils, markers, stencils, pens, pencils, erasers, and other art materials. These items can turn your map into a work of art!

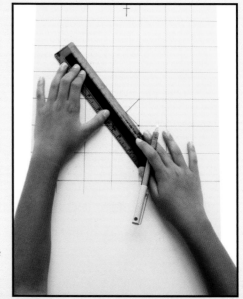

A grid ensures that you will place items on your map in the right spot.

Correct measurements are extremely important if you want your map to be accurate. A calculator can help you determine scale.

Mapping the Basics

Now you have the purpose, the data, and the tools for your map. It is time to start creating the map! Making the base map is the first step. The base map is like your map's skeleton. It shows just an area's borders and main features. This might mean the walls, the doors, and the windows in your bedroom. Or, it might be the outlines of state boundaries on a U.S. map.

For a small area, a **cartographer** might create a new base map. For large areas, base maps are often copied from books or downloaded from the Internet. Once the map's boundaries are set, other information can be added.

A good base map is the foundation for any type of map. Remember, accurate distances and shapes help truthfully show the information you want to communicate.

A blueprint is a kind of base map, too. If you wanted to map each room of your house, a blueprint would help you determine where to place the furniture.

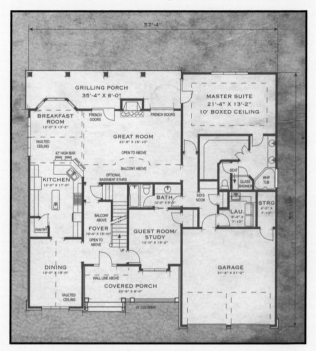

But first, it is important to orient the map. Orientation helps people who read the map know which way to go. So, the base map should have an arrow that indicates which way is north. The arrow is often marked with an *N* or the word *North.* Usually, the arrow points to the top of the map.

You could also add a compass rose to your map. This is another symbol that shows direction. A compass rose often looks like a star or a flower, which is why it is called a rose. It can have four, eight, or more petals.

The four largest petals point to the cardinal directions, which are north, south, east, and west. The north petal is marked. On older maps, a flower symbol called a fleur-de-lis (fluhr-duh-LEE) was often used. Smaller petals point to intermediate directions. These are northeast, northwest, southeast, and southwest.

Latitude and longitude form a grid system. These lines intersect to help locate places on Earth.

Sometimes, base maps also have a grid. This is a system of **intersecting** lines that help the reader find things. A grid also helps the mapmaker **accurately** place things on the map. City maps sometimes use a grid labeled with numbers and letters.

Small-**scale** base maps also need a **projection**. This is the method **cartographers** use to display the round world on a flat map. Different projections **distort** what is being mapped in a variety of ways. So, the mapmaker must choose a projection that suits the map's purpose.

For example, a **cylindrical projection** known as the Mercator projection is important for navigation. This is because it shows true direction. But, this projection **distorts** the size and the shape of areas far from the equator.

No one projection can map the whole world **accurately**. But if you want to map the United States, a **conical** projection is best. This type of projection does not distort the midlatitude areas where North America lies.

A

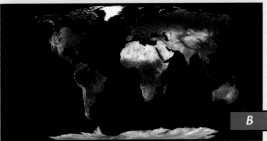

B

C

Sizing Up Scale

Next, you must determine your map's **scale**. **Cartographers** begin by finding the length and width of the area to be mapped. Then, they determine how to fit the area onto the map. To do this, they divide the longest length of the area by the longest side of the paper. This shows how many inches in reality are represented by each inch on the map.

There are three types of map scales. A word scale is a statement such as "one inch equals one mile." A representative fraction (RF) scale is a fraction. The RF 1:100 means 1 unit on the map equals 100 units in reality. Both sides of an RF scale must refer to the same type of unit. So, 1:10 can mean 1 inch (3 cm) equals 10 inches (25 cm). It cannot mean 1 inch equals 10 feet (3 m).

A bar **scale** is like a small ruler drawn on a map. It shows a length that can be measured against any area on the map. The bar scale is the only scale that remains **accurate** if a map is enlarged or reduced in size. This is because the bar changes size with the map. RF scales and word scales must be recalculated if the map size changes.

Finding Scale

Imagine your classroom is 360 inches (914 cm) long. But, your paper is only 12 inches (30 cm) long. How many inches in the classroom should each inch on the paper represent?

First, calculate the scale. If you leave a 1-inch (3-cm) border, your map will be 10 inches (25 cm) wide. Divide the length of the room, 360, by the length of the map, 10. The answer is 36. So, each inch on the map will represent 36 inches (91 cm) in the classroom.

A word scale for this map would read "one inch equals 36 inches." The RF scale is 1:36. This is because one inch on the map equals 36 inches in the classroom. For a bar scale, draw a line one inch long using a ruler. Below the line write "36 inches."

word scale	one inch equals 36 inches
representative fraction	1:36
bar scale	36 0 18 36 72 (in inches) 1 inch = 36 inches

Design Details

Don't be afraid to make your map your own creation! Bright colors make this map cheerful and fun.

Cartographers must be **accurate**. But, making their maps easy to understand is equally important. Keep this in mind when choosing your map's design elements.

Cartographers try to choose colors that are easy to interpret. Most people would say blue should represent water and green should represent **vegetation**. You do not have to use these colors. But, your map's colors should be pleasing and distinctive.

Symbols on a map should also be easy to understand. For example, it would be confusing if little tree symbols represented buildings. Many symbols clearly show what they stand for. Less obvious symbols can be looked up in a chart called a legend.

Often, symbols are shown in different sizes. For example, a big circle might represent a state capital, while smaller circles represent other cities. To avoid confusion, all objects that are the same should be represented with the same symbol.

Labels also help identify objects on a map, such as city or road names. It is important that the labels are easy to read. Too many labels can make a map look messy!

Finally, the **cartographer** adds the legend to the map. This is a list of what each symbol or color means. The legend will help people understand all the information on the map.

Choose your labels wisely. On a map of your bedroom, labels might include your bed, dresser, and any other pieces of furniture. A globe should include labels for every country without jumbling the words together. For some parts of the world, this would be a tricky job!

Reference Maps

Now it's time to make the map! For reference maps, the **cartographer** places the largest and most important elements on the map first. Then, he or she carefully measures how far each object is from the map's boundaries. If the map has a grid, the cartographer can **accurately** place additional features using the grid lines.

For example, a cartographer mapping a city might begin by outlining the city's boundaries. Then he or she would add any large buildings, monuments, roads, and parks. The grid helps the cartographer make sure every item is sized in relation to other objects on the map. Once large items are placed, smaller details can be added.

Perhaps you want to create a map of your classroom. You should begin with the teacher's desk. If the map has a 1:36 RF **scale**, be sure to position the desk according to that scale. So if the desk is 36 inches (91 cm) from the wall in reality, it must be placed one inch (3 cm) from the wall on the map. After the desk is in the right spot, you might add the student desks and so on.

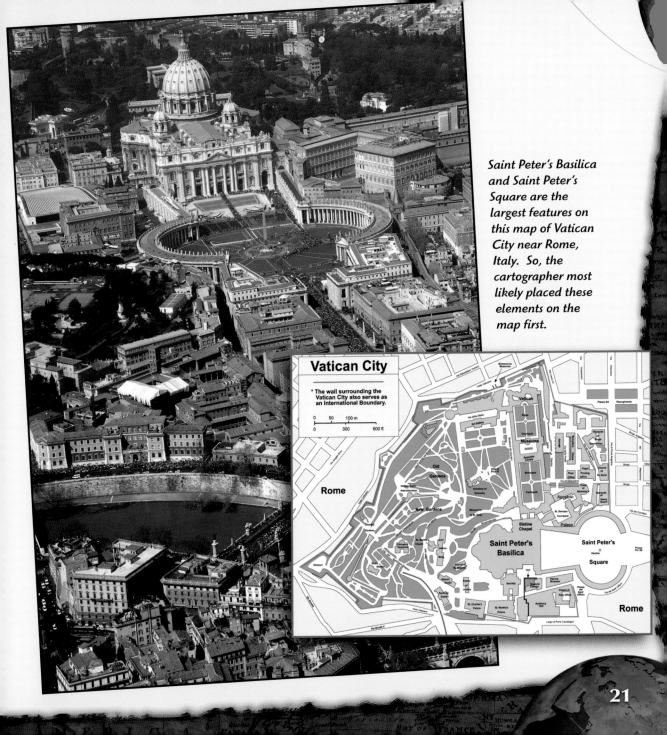

Saint Peter's Basilica and Saint Peter's Square are the largest features on this map of Vatican City near Rome, Italy. So, the cartographer most likely placed these elements on the map first.

Vatican City

* The wall surrounding the Vatican City also serves as an International Boundary.

0   50   100 m

0   300   600 ft

Rome

Old Gardens

New Gardens

Vatican

Museums

Sistine Chapel

Apostolic

Palace

Saint Peter's Basilica

Saint Peter's Square

Rome

Thematic Maps

Thematic maps compare data across an area. They can show differences or similarities. Although thematic maps are not used for navigation, **scale** and **projection** are still important. Maps not drawn to scale or with unsuitable projections can misrepresent the data.

To make a thematic map, a **cartographer** divides the data into cohorts. For example, hair color may have cohorts of Black, Brown, Red, Blond, or Other. People who believe in UFOs may be divided into three cohorts of Yes, No, and No Opinion. Cohorts also can represent percentages.

Thematic maps often have a category for the unknown. This is because everyone in a survey must be accounted for. Sometimes, people in the surveyed group have no opinion or are absent. So, they are mapped in the Unknown cohort.

Finally, the cartographer assigns a color or a symbol to each cohort. These are recorded in the map's legend. Then, each area in the map is filled with the colors or symbols showing what it represents.

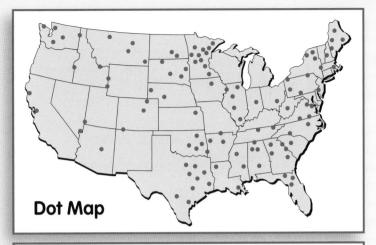

Dot Map

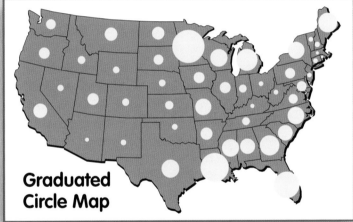

Graduated Circle Map

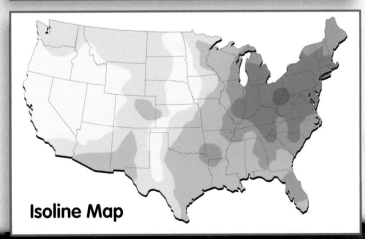

Isoline Map

Symbols

Thematic maps often use symbols to communicate information. Dots, graduated circles, and isolines are common symbols.

On a dot map, each dot represents a certain number. These are often used for population maps. For example, each dot might represent 1,000 people. Dots also show distribution, such as how crowded an area is.

On a graduated circle map, the size of the circle shows proportion. For example, big circles might represent large cities, while small circles represent towns.

Isolines are a thematic symbol that connect areas that are equal. These lines are used to show continuous distributions. For example, isotherms show areas of equal temperature on a weather map. Isolines can also show changes in elevation.

Finishing the Map

The map isn't finished quite yet! It still needs a title, a date, and a source. Titles are usually placed at the top or the bottom of the map. The title reveals the purpose of the map.

The source and the date can be written in a corner or on the back of the map. They tell the reader who created the map and when the information was collected. Any data that was collected from other sources should also be noted.

Neatness and creativity add interest to a map. For instance, many maps have decorative borders. Pictures may be drawn or painted in empty areas. And, fancy lettering may be used for titles and legends. A beautiful map makes people want to explore the information it presents.

Maps are often displayed on walls like pictures. This is because mapmaking is not just a science. A well-made map is a work of art!

Many old maps have detailed decorations that fill areas that were still unexplored at the time of their making.

Modern Mapping

Cartographers have been making maps by hand for centuries. But today, computers make mapping faster and easier. Some computer mapping programs are simple enough for students to use. To create **complex** maps, professionals often use computer-aided-design (CAD) programs.

Geographic Information Systems (GISs) combine a mapping program with tools that collect, store, and **analyze** data. The software allows many maps to be combined together in layers, like a sandwich. These systems help people make better decisions about how to use or protect an area. City planners can monitor population growth over time or determine the best way to use land.

GIS technology can help community officials determine where to provide services.

Having a GPS device in your car is a great way to get out and explore! The system provides real-time navigation while you are on the road.

Inventions such as the **Global Positioning System (GPS) satellites** allow real-time tracking. This means that objects on a map display can be tracked as they move. These systems are used in cars to guide drivers while they are on the road.

Computer cartographers design and create thousands of maps! Some can be viewed on the Internet.

Computer **cartographers** follow traditional mapmaking principles. Maps must still have a purpose and be thoughtfully designed. Thematic map data must be **analyzed**. Reference map information must be gathered carefully. And, choices must be made as to what goes on the map. Care must always be taken to **accurately** place objects.

Computers help gather and combine large amounts of information. They allow mapmakers to experiment with different symbols, colors, and writing styles. And, maps can be updated quickly with new information.

Today, technology makes it possible for almost anyone to make maps. This can be a powerful way to communicate information about your world to other people. Yet, it will always take scientific **accuracy** and an artist's eye to make a great map!

Glossary

accurate - free of errors.

analyze - to determine the meaning of something by breaking down its parts. An analyst is a person who analyzes.

cartographer - a maker of maps or charts.

complex - having many parts, details, ideas, or functions.

conical - shaped like a cone.

cylindrical - shaped like a cylinder. A cylinder is a solid figure of two parallel circles bound by a curved surface. A soda can is an example of a cylinder.

distort - to change or misrepresent the normal shape or condition of something.

durable - able to exist for a long time without weakening.

Global Positioning System (GPS) - a network of transmitters and satellite signals that work together to pinpoint locations for navigation and tracking.

intersect - to meet and cross at one or more points.

projection - the representation, upon a flat surface, of all or part of the surface of the earth or another celestial sphere.

satellite - a manufactured object that orbits Earth.

scale - the size of a map, a drawing, or a model compared with what it represents. Also, the equally divided line on a map or a chart that indicates this relationship.

statistic - a quantity that is calculated from a sample.

vegetation - plant life.

Web Sites

To learn more about cartography, visit ABDO Publishing Company on the World Wide Web at **www.abdopublishing.com**. Web sites about cartography are featured on our Book Links page. These links are routinely monitored and updated to provide the most current information available.

Index